This Book Belongs To

_____

Little Allies

By Julie Kratz
illustrations by Edward Maiello

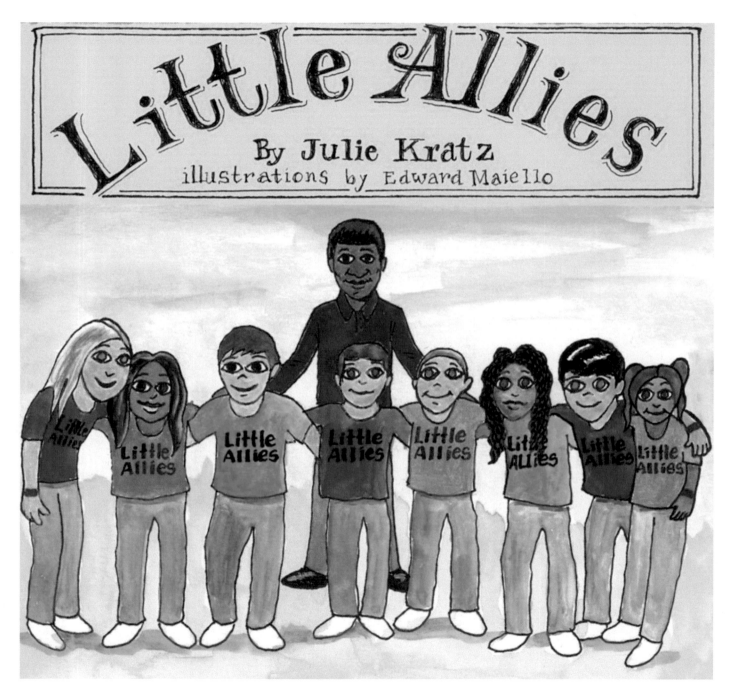

Next Pivot Point Publishing

Books may be ordered through booksellers or by contacting:

Julie Kratz
Next Pivot Point Publishing
Julie@nextpivotpoint.com

TheLittleAllies.com
317-525-4310

13470 Shakamac Drive
Carmel, IN 46032

ISBN: 978-1-7365159-0-7 (paperback)
ISBN: 978-1-7365159-1-4 (eBook)

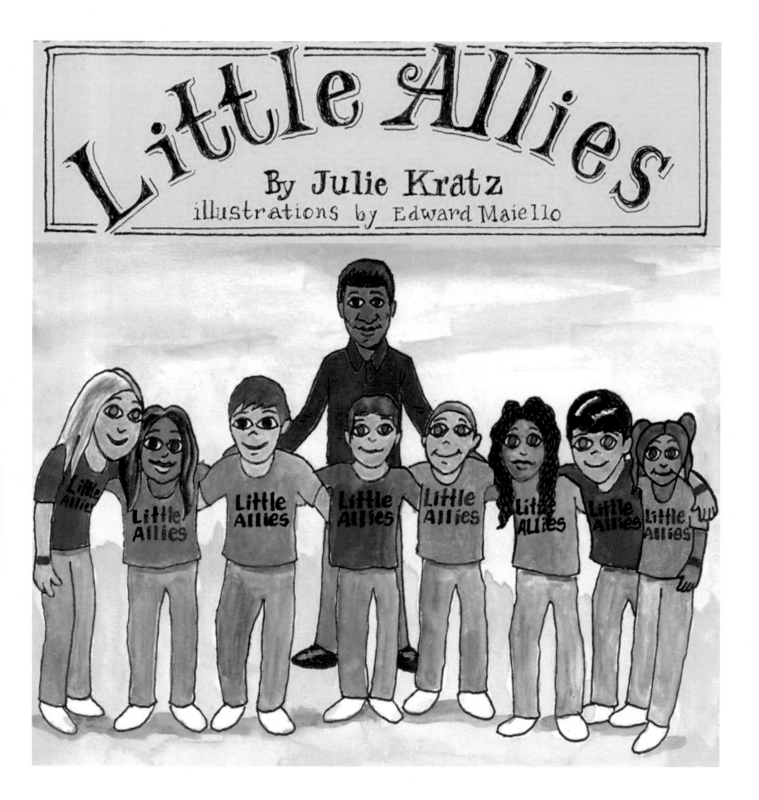

Hi, my name is Ally Rogers. I am in Mr. Clark's fourth grade class at Friendship Elementary.

I love school, especially math and science. But what I love the most is playing with my friends on the playground.

I learned something really important this week.

It all began on Monday during recess when I was playing tag with Prisha and Tommy.

Tommy chased us around the swings, pointed at Prisha and said, "You don't belong here."

Prisha stopped running and turned to Tommy. "Why don't I belong?"

Tommy said. "You are different. You are not from here."

You see, last week, Prisha brought in Indian clothes for show and tell.

It was really cool to learn about her family. They have a special festival called Diwali. It is as important to them as Christmas is to my family.

Did Tommy think Prisha didn't belong because her family was from India? This made me feel weird.

I didn't know what to do. Tommy hurt Prisha's feelings and I wanted to make her feel better.

What would you do?

Finally, I said to Tommy, "Prisha is my friend. She belongs as much as I do. She is fun to play with and I like learning about India and her family."

I think Tommy was surprised because he just stood there looking at us.

Once we were back in class, Tommy did something neither of us expected.

Tommy said, "I'm sorry, I didn't mean to say that. But I don't understand why you don't celebrate Christmas. Everyone I know celebrates Christmas."

Tommy's apology helped Prisha feel better. She was even brave enough to tell him more about Diwali.

"Diwali is a lot like your Christmas. We celebrate as a family and light diyas, that are like candles. Diyas outshine the darkness. Like your Christmas, it is a special time for my family."

It was amazing. I watched two kids become friends right before my eyes!

Tommy and Prisha's new friendship was not all that happened this week. Let me tell you about my friend Henry.

On Tuesday before language arts class, my friend Henry looked a bit confused. So, I asked, "Henry, are you okay?"

You see, I knew Henry was supposed to go to his special day class while we had reading. His teacher must have been late meeting him.

Henry nodded. "I am okay." He didn't look okay, he looked scared.

Henry looked like he needed a friend. I asked, "Henry, what is it like to go to your special day classes?"

Henry's face lit up. "I *love* going to my special classes. My teacher says that I have special powers!"

I'm so glad I waited with him. Instead of being scared, Henry was excited to tell me all about his class. Now, I wait with him every day and he tells me funny stories.

This is how I see Henry now.

On Wednesday during snack time, Mr. Clark read a story. It was about different jobs like firefighters and bankers. Then he asked us to share where our parents worked.

This sounds like a regular day at school, right? Well, it wasn't. It was a really big deal. Let me tell you about my friend Jack.

Jack raised his hand. When Mr. Clark called on him he said, "My moms are both doctors."

"Both your moms?" Prisha asked. She was probably thinking Jack just said it wrong.

Jack said with a huge smile. "Yep, both of them. They are the best moms in the world!"

Jack is my friend. He invited me to his birthday party this summer. I learned that instead of having both a mom and a dad, Jack has two moms. Isn't that cool?

Yasmine pulled on Jack's pant leg. "What about your dad? How does he feel about two moms?" The whole class watched quietly, confused.

"I don't have a dad. My moms are my parents." Jack said, sitting back down. His smile was gone.

A few of the kids looked at each other, surprised. You know what I thought? This was just like what happened between Prisha and Tommy on the playground. My friends needed to learn more about Jack's family to understand.

Mr. Clark knew just what to say. I was glad because I was too shy to say something with the whole class listening.

"Every family is different, and isn't that what makes each one special? What is most important is that families are filled with love. Thank you for sharing about your parents Jack. I bet they know how important it is to do your homework *and* to eat your broccoli."

The whole class groaned. I guess they don't really like homework or broccoli.

On Thursday, I spent some time with my friend Lucia. Lucia and I like to color together during free time. Her family is from Mexico and she speaks another language. Isn't that cool? I only speak English, but Lucia is so smart she speaks Spanish too.

Sometimes kids tease Lucia because she doesn't always know the English words. I think this is why she is quiet in school.

Lucia told me she likes when I help her find the right words when we sit and color. I love it when she teaches me Spanish words!

Later in PE class, Coach asked us to line up. The girls were on one side and the boys on the other side.

My friend Sam stood in the middle of the gym looking from one side to the other. Coach pointed for Sam to join the boys side.

What Coach didn't realize was that Sam did not identify as a boy or a girl. Sam had explained to me that this is known as gender non-binary. Sam looked really scared. So, I stood next to Sam for support. Coach looked confused.

Then Coach announced, "Kids born between January and June on my left. Those born in July through December on my right."

We were on the same team now! I was so happy Coach knew how to make Sam feel more included.

Sam walked past the coach and smiled. "Thanks Coach."

You're probably wondering when I'm going to tell you what I learned. I'm almost there, just let me tell you about my friend Yasmine.

Last week we had twin day. We were supposed to dress up like another kid in our class. Yasmine and I decided to be twins. We both have long hair, the same pink shirt, and royal crowns from our matching Halloween costumes.

Remember Tommy from Monday's story? Well, he didn't have a twin. I guess he wasn't as excited about twin day as some of my friends.

When Mr. Clark was taking our picture, Tommy asked, "Ally, who are you supposed to be twins with?"

I looked at him like he had three heads and pointed at Yasmine. We even wore *matching* sneakers and jeans. From head to toe, we matched!

"You can't be twins. Yasmine is nothing like you. She's Black."

I was so glad Yasmine knew what to say to Tommy because I did not.

Yasmine said, "Tommy, we know we don't look exactly alike. How could we? Nobody is exactly the same as anyone else."

Tommy looked confused.

Yasmine continued, "My skin and hair are beautiful, and so are Ally's. We can be twins because we are both beautiful and smart."

I still felt really weird about what Tommy said. But I didn't know how to make it better. I wanted to say Yasmine is exactly like me. She is smart, brave, and my best friend. Her black skin didn't change any of that.

Thankfully, Mr. Clark said something that helped all of us. "It's okay to call someone Black, Tommy. What is not okay is if you say it in a way that makes someone feel they are less because of the color of their skin."

Tommy must have felt bad because I saw tears in his eyes. "I'm sorry Yasmine. I didn't mean to hurt your feelings. Now that I think about it you and Ally are a lot alike."

This is the part I've been waiting to tell you about!

I promise all of my stories will make sense in a minute.

Every Friday Mr. Clark asks us to share what we have learned during the week.

For once, I am ready with my answer!

Mr. Clark said, "Class, let's share what we've learned this week. Do we have any volunteers?"

I raised my hand.

Mr. Clark pointed at me, "Ally, why don't you tell us what you've learned."

"I learned that my friends aren't exactly like me. They're unique and different. I think that makes all of us more interesting."

Mr. Clark nodded, "That's really good Ally. Tell us more."

"We all have different abilities, skin colors, and religions. Some of us have different kinds of families, or speak different languages."

"Our differences make us unique and special, but we are all kids who like to have fun together. We all like to play hide and seek on the playground. We like to eat lunch and laugh. We want to have friends and tell jokes."

I took a deep breath. That was the most I ever said in front of the class.

I sat back down. My face felt weirdly hot. I don't like to talk in front of the class, but I had something important to share.

Then Mr. Clark said something really cool. "Did you know that Ally's name also has another meaning? It's spelled the same, but you say it like this - *Al-eye.* Do you know what that word means?"

Everyone was quiet.

"An ally is someone who helps others who are different. An ally is there for you when you are teased. Or when someone treats you unfairly. It can be a teacher, a parent, or a friend. Does that make sense?"

Everyone looked a bit confused. Even me.

Mr. Clark said, "It is funny. Ally taught us something important today. We can see how we are different. But that doesn't mean we have to treat people differently."

Then he asked, "How can you be an ally to kids who are different from you?"

I decided right then that I'm committing to being an ally to my classmates. I will listen and learn more about them.

When I know more about my friends, I can see how alike we really are. This makes me a better friend and an ally to everyone.

The Ally Promise

- I believe in equality.

- I commit to being an ally for others.

- I want to be there for people that are different from me.

- I ask questions in a way that is respectful.

- I am curious.

- I empathize with others.

- I listen to learn more.

Visit TheLittleAllies.com to download your printable My Ally Promise agreement!

Caregiver, Parent, and Educator Discussion Guide*

1. What is one new thing you learned in the story?

2. What character(s) do you identify with most?

3. When Tommy said Prisha did not belong, how do you think that made Prisha feel?

4. When Ally sat with Lucia, she let Lucia know she was there for her but didn't make her feel uncomfortable by asking a lot of questions. What are some other examples in the book where Ally was a quiet ally to her classmates?

5. Name a few ways Ally showed she values her classmate's differences.

6. Name a few ways that you could stick up for a classmate when another child is being unkind or unfairly treating others because they are different?

7. How can you learn more about kids who are different from you? How do you think knowing more about a friend can help you be a better ally?

8. What goals could you set to help your classmates and the challenges they face?

Visit TheLittleAllies.com to download your printable Discussion Guide.

Terms to Know

Learning the correct language to talk about (and celebrate!) our differences is an important step towards being an ally to others. Below are some terms to start with and remember, you should always keep learning and adding more terms to your inclusive dictionary! *

- **Ally**: One that leverages their privilege to help others that are underrepresented (i.e., mentor, sponsor, advocate, coach, challenger)
- **Diversity**: Different groups of people (i.e., gender, race, ethnicity, sexual orientation, abilities)
- **Inclusion**: A sense of belonging for diverse groups of people
- **Intersectionality**: The intersection of more than one marker of diversity (i.e., race + gender, disabled + gay)
- **Gender non-binary**: A category for those that identify outside of the masculine or feminine gender boxes (synonym: gender-neutral)
- **Cisgender**: A category for those that identify their gender with the gender or sex they were assigned at birth
- **LGBTQ+**: An acronym that represents lesbian, gay, bisexual, transgender, queer and those that identify with other markers of difference in sexual orientation and/or gender
- **People of color**: People that identify as non-white
- **Disabilities**: Physical or non-physical differences from the majority group (i.e., mental health, limited mobility, visually impaired)
- **Privilege**: The advantages one has over others based on their associations with the majority group (i.e., white, straight, male, cisgender, able-bodied)
- **Gender equality**: The belief that all genders of humans are equal and should be treated equally.

Download the full diversity dictionary at Nextpivotpoint.com.

About the Author

Julie Kratz is a highly acclaimed TEDx speaker and inclusive leadership trainer who led teams and produced results in corporate America. After experiencing many career "pivot points" of her own, she started her own speaking business focused on helping leaders be more inclusive.

Promoting diversity and inclusion in the workplace, Julie is a frequent keynote speaker, podcast host, and executive coach. She holds an MBA from the Kelley School of Business at Indiana University, is a Certified Master Coach, and is a certified unconscious bias trainer.

Meet Julie at NextPivotPoint.com and **TheLittleAllies.com**.

Other Books by Julie Kratz

Pivot Point: How to Build a Winning Career Game Plan,

ONE: How Male Allies Support Women for Gender Equality,

Lead Like an Ally: A Journey Through Corporate America with Strategies to Facilitate Inclusion

Made in the USA
Coppell, TX
09 June 2021